CW00493130

This book is dedicated to my wife, my rock, my forever friend and partner in crime. Nothing would be possible without your continuous love and support.

Quarto is the authority on a wide range of topics.

Quarto educates, entertains and enriches the lives of our readers—enthusiasts and lovers of hands-on living.

www.quartoknows.com

© 2015 Quarto Publishing Group USA Inc.

Artwork © 2016 Ryan McArthur

Text © 2016 Quarto Publishing Group USA

Interior Design: Monica Gurevich-Importico

First published in the United States of America in 2016 by
Rock Point Publishing, a member of
Quarto Publishing Group USA Inc.
142 West 36th Street, 4th Floor
New York, NY 10018
quartoknows.com
Visit our blogs at quartoknows.com

10 9 8 7 6 5 4 3 2 1

ISBN: 978-1-63106-166-0

Printed in China

ARTFULLY SPOKEN

30 Beautifully Illustrated Life-Changing Quotations

Illustrative Works by Ryan McArthur

ROCKPOINT
QUARTOKNOWS.COM

THIS QUOTE CHALLENGES PEOPLE to worry less about how long they will live and more about if they are living well. One of the most-quoted American writers in history, Ralph Waldo Emerson lost much of his writing to a house fire in his late sixties. Not wanting the rest to be lost, he collected together old poems, and correspondence and published them in an expansive ten-volume set. Volume eight included the essay "Immortality," where this quote is from.

While most of us don't have ten volumes of wisdom and literature in us, we do have the ability to enrich our lives with worthy pursuits. This passage from "Immortality" continues: "It is not duration, but a taking of the soul out of time, as all high action of the mind does: when we are living in the sentiments we ask no questions about time." Catching up with an old friend, meditating, even rigorous debate can be "high actions of the mind" that suspend time and help us get lost in the moment. Remember the important moments that bring meaningful depth to your life.

RALPH
EMERSON

IT'S
NOT THE
LENGTH
OF LIFE
BUT THE
DEPTH
OF LIFE.

JUST AS A BIKE WHEEL will travel through many rough spots over the course of its life, so too will you! Steady yourself, and keep pedaling. If you dwell too long on the bumps in the road, you'll never get anywhere.

One of history's most brilliant thinkers, Albert Einstein immigrated to the United States in 1933 to escape the regime of Adolf Hitler, and didn't let the fact that his books were burned in his home country keep him from continuing to speak out. He also continued to publish scientific papers and work on this theories—some, which worked out, and some, which didn't. Einstein championed the right to free speech, and credited his creativity to this lifelong belief in individual liberty. He continued to evolve throughout his life, even bringing the speech he was working on to the hospital with him on the day he passed away. Not only are his remarkable theories still learned and examined by modern scientists, but his image as an "everyman" who believed that anyone could be a great thinker persists and enlightens us to this day. What will you think up if you're able to pedal past the rough patches?

Life is like riding a bicycle.

To keep your balance, you must keep moving.

STAY TRUE TO YOURSELF! It can be harder than it sounds. Perhaps because it can be scary to present our true selves to the world, but also because it can be even more difficult to know ourselves and what we want out of life. As we struggle to find the self within, it is important to remember not to become a "carbon copy" of those who are successful around us.

Edward Young, an often-struggling English writer, was best known for his epic poem *Night Thoughts*. In it, he laments the deaths of his loved ones, including his wife and daughter. Life is short, and Young wanted no one to waste it. "Procrastination is the thief of time," he wrote in the poem. Once you discover who your true self is, don't waste any time letting it show!

We are all born originals,

why is it so many of us die copies?

NO MATTER HOW SHORT, long, happy, sad, simple, or vast—each of us has a story to tell. Fyodor Dostoyevsky, widely regarded as one of the best writers to ever live, was particularly interested in the story that each person had to tell. He especially focused on people who were marginalized by society, like the poor, and even murderers. Instead of sensationalizing them, Dostoyevsky tried to understand these people, looking for the humanity behind their actions.

Dostoyevsky himself didn't lead an easy life. Born in Russia in 1821, he lived on the grounds of a hospital for the poor that employed his father, a surgeon. Later, he was imprisoned in a Siberian labor camp for reading essays that were critical of the Russian government. Perhaps it was these hardships that allowed him to be empathetic to those around him, even those who received no sympathy from others. It's this quality that makes his novels touch people's souls to this day. What is your story?

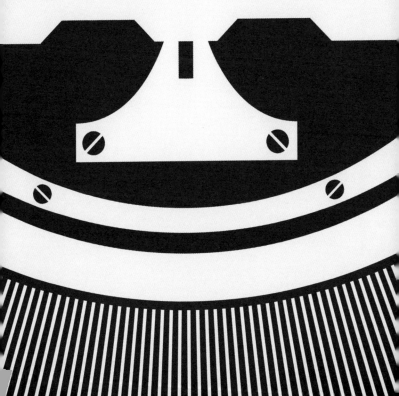

FYODOR
DOSTOYEVSKY

But how could you live and have no story to tell?

THOMAS JEFFERSON, the primary author of the Declaration of Independence, the third president of the United States, and one of the most respected writers and orators in American history, certainly knew the value of books. We are the sum of our parts, and what better building blocks than books? Jefferson was an avid book collector throughout his life, and was said to have had more than 6,500 books in his personal library at the time of his death, including works about ancient and modern history, philosophy, and even plays and poetry.

Jefferson used these books to inform his philosophies about our "unalienable rights" as humans, lead the people, and become one of the most important figures in early America. Reading is so much more than fact-finding and inspiration. The author C.S. Lewis once said, "We read to know we are not alone." In characters both fictional and real, we see ourselves, and by reading their stories, we better understand our own. Make sure not to live without books.

THOMAS JEFFERSON

I cannot live without books.

THIS FAMOUS QUOTE ABOUT HARD WORK challenges you to put in the needed effort after having a great idea. Thomas Edison definitely wasn't lacking great ideas. After inventing the light bulb we know today, he developed a system to get that light, via electricity, into homes. He also invented the first video camera, made advances in recording music, and—way ahead of his time—invented a battery-operated electric car. Edison was successful not only because of his great ideas, but also because of the time he devoted developing them. He took no shame in perfecting the work of other people, saying, "My principal business consists of giving commercial value to the brilliant, but misdirected, ideas of others." Edison was able to find practical use in lofty ideas thanks to the time he put into listening to those around him, learning the market, and using trial and error. All in all, Edison ended up holding 1,093 US patents in his name, and he perspired for every one. Just like the old adage says, nothing worth having comes easy.

*Genius is one percent inspiration
and ninety-nine percent perspiration.*

IN THIS QUOTE, NOVELIST WILLIAM THACKERAY urges each of us to be the best we can be. Thackeray was a writer best known for his satirical novel *Vanity Fair*. Although this quote is often misattributed to Abraham Lincoln, it comes from the autobiography of magazine editor Laurence Hutton, who met Thackeray when Hutton was a young boy. After asking Thackeray's advice as to what he should be when he grows up, Thackeray places his hand on Hutton's head and tells him, "Whatever you are, try to be a good one." In the intervening century, the "try to" has dropped out.

Very often your path in life isn't clear and you will find yourself looking for direction. Your journey of self-discovery is about more than hitting milestones or attaining notable achievements; it is about paying close attention to what you are doing now, with that focus you will find your unique, true self. So often *what* you do is not as important as *how* you do it. In order to lead a happy life it is fundamentally important to embrace life both the large moments and the small with gusto and passion, wherever they take you.

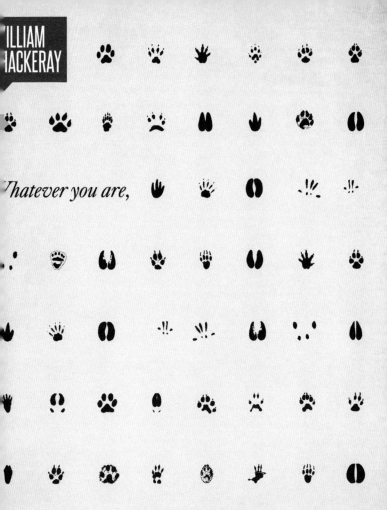

Whatever you are,

be a good one.

WHETHER IT'S THE STRUM OF A GUITAR, the lifting of a voice, or even the beautiful green of grass, it's the little things that make life worthwhile. "How little is required for happiness!" Nietzsche wrote right before this quotation from his book *Twilight of the Idols*. Considered one of the fathers of postmodern philosophy, Nietzsche spent much time pondering the meaning of life, religion, and morality.

Like many of us, Nietzsche spent his life battling demons, both mental and physical. He suffered from days-long migraine headaches from a young age, vision deterioration that led to blindness, depression, and delusions. Although he had a promising career as the chair of the Classical philosophy department at Switzerland's prestigious University of Basel, he was forced to retire at the age of 34 due to his health problems. Still, he continued to write, and these writings have lived on to inspire some of the world's most famous poets, psychologists, and free-thinkers. One wonders what music Nietzsche drew his inspiration from. Where will you draw yours?

FRIEDRICH
NIETZSCHE

Without music, life would be a mistake.

THIS EXISTENTIAL QUOTE by Persian theologian Jalal ad-Din Muhammad Rumi (usually just called "Rumi") challenges you to connect to the great and wonderful world around you by starting within.

Rumi was one of the greatest scholars and teachers of Sufism, which encourages people to get closer to God by abandoning their egos (or false personalities) and focusing on personal and community development. Sufis believe in trying to connect oneself to the constant motion of the body (the breath in our lungs, the moving of blood in our veins, even the revolution of molecules and the atoms inside them), and one such way is through dancing. The whirling dervishes, a ritual dance that Rumi developed, allow the dervishes (similar to monks) to consciously revolve like their bodies naturally do, thereby finding harmony with the world around them and communing with God. Rumi hoped that, through the movement and music, people would find their inner truths and emerge from the dance with a greater ability to help their fellow man, no matter what their race, beliefs, or differences. What will you bring to the world around you after you look inside to find the ocean within?

*You
are not a
drop in the ocean.*

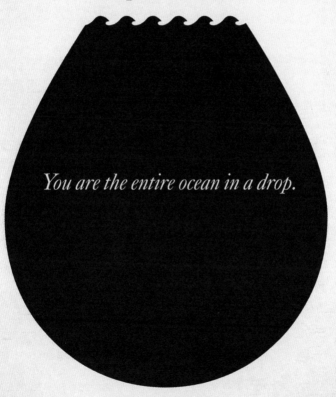

You are the entire ocean in a drop.

EVEN IF SOMETHING SEEMS IMPOSSIBLE, having a little faith will bring an unexpected piece to help fill your need. Mary McLeod Bethune was filled with faith throughout her entire life. Born the child of former slaves in Mayesville, South Carolina, just after the Civil War, she relentlessly pursued an education and a God-filled life to become a groundbreaking teacher, human rights advocate, and adviser to five different presidents. Even as a small child, Mary wanted to read, and when a Presbyterian school for African-American children opened four miles from her home when she was around ten years old, she was eager to attend. She later earned scholarships to further her schooling, and soon opened a school herself, even though she relied mostly on donations from church and community members. Although the school started out using boxes for chairs and packing crates for desks, it went on to receive donations from the likes of John D. Rockefeller, and Bethune went on to hold the then-highest government position of any black American, as an advisor to Franklin Roosevelt. Even in the darkest times, it is so important to keep faith in who you are.

Without faith, nothing is possible.
With it, nothing is impossible.

JUST AS THE BEAUTY OF THE SUN ATTRACTS A beautiful seed to grow and blossom toward it, if we put beauty into the world, we will find ourselves surrounded with beauty.

A poet of the Romantic period of the early 1800s, Leigh Hunt was known for his sunny personality, love of conversation, and lively demeanor. He was well-loved by his friends, and gave personal advice and inspiration to some of the greatest poets and writers to ever live, including John Keats, Robert Browning, Charles Dickens, and Alfred, Lord Tennyson. It was said that no one who knew him did not love him, and his generosity of spirit also made him a fair and impartial literary critic. Leigh Hunt's poems are filled with lyrical descriptions of nature, which inspired him to delight those around him, and in turn, the world. So go ahead, take a walk. Plant a seed. See if it finds the sun.

The beautiful

attracts the beautiful.

PEOPLE WILL ALWAYS DEBATE the question of whether everything in this world is in our control, completely out of our control, or somewhere in between.

Ralph Waldo Emerson pondered these thoughts as one of the founders of individualism, the philosophical idea that it's important for everyone to be their own person, no matter who that person might be. Emerson believed that, "Whoso would be a man, must be a nonconformist"—that people could not fully grow if they are just repeating the thoughts, actions, and ideas of the society around them.

A dear friend of Emerson's was Henry David Thoreau, who took Emerson's philosophies on individualism so to heart that he went to live on Emerson's property by the shores of Walden Pond, alone with nature for two years. By being self-reliant, away from society, Thoreau was able to focus on his personal development, and valued wisdom over money and success. When no one was interested in his essay on his time spent at Walden Pond, he published it himself, and it's now known as one of the greatest works about finding inner peace through nature ever written. What decisions will you make when you allow yourself to become who you truly are?

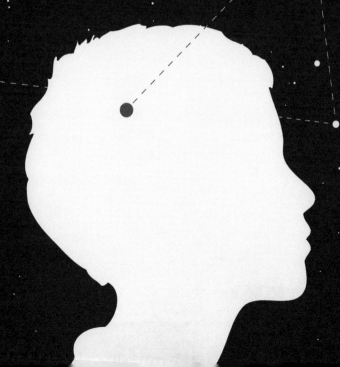

Once you make a decision,
the universe conspires to make it happen.

RALPH
EMERSON

WITH THIS QUOTE, philosopher Albert Camus challenges us to go out into the world to experience all it has to offer, and commit fully to the ups and downs that come with it. Camus loved paradoxes, and believed that one reason we're able to enjoy life so much is because we won't live forever. Best known as the writer of such novels as *The Plague* and *The Stranger*, he often covered the theme of how hard it can be to find meaning in a world that often seems to offer few answers. However, he never stopped searching. When he won the Nobel Prize for Literature in 1957, the Nobel committee commended his "clear-sighted earnestness [that] illuminates the problems of the human conscience in our times." Camus would die in a car accident three years later at the age of 42. Still, during that short time, he accomplished much. Born into poverty, he worked odd jobs to get by; founded a theatre company; fought for human rights; and published more than a dozen books, including novels, short stories, plays, and essays. Camus never waited for life to happen to him—he met it head on, challenged it, and underwent experiences that gave him a depth far beyond his 42 years. Go out into the world and explore.

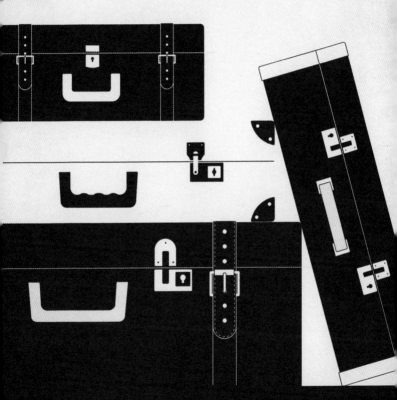

ALBERT CAMUS

You cannot create experience.

You must undergo it.

WOULDN'T IT BE NICE if we could just erase things from the past and start over fresh? Unfortunately, life is rarely that easy. But you can approach life in a positive way that emphasizes the future over the past.

John W. Gardner was someone who lived his life in just such a way. A former Marine captain and head of the US Department of Health, Education, and Welfare, he also counseled six US presidents, was a leader in the fight for civil rights and education reform, and received the Presidential Award of Freedom. Throughout it all, he kept a positive attitude that not only impressed, but positively impacted those around him. A reporter once noted, "It is not difficult to tell what Mr. Gardner has done. It is more daunting to describe how he does it. In Mr. Gardner, you experience the best kind of citizen and leader—optimistic, positive, curious, open….No matter how good you feel when you are on your way to meet him, you are going to feel better when you leave." If you can inspire that kind of joy in those around you, who needs an eraser?

*Life is the art of drawing
without an eraser.*

EACH YEAR A TREE IS ALIVE, it grows another outer layer around its trunk, leading to rings on the inside that indicate its age. People also have years of layers, mapping our history. Just as the laws of nature require that a tree live a whole year before another layer is formed, we too must be patient with our own development in putting down roots and growing tall.

One of the largest accomplishments of Samuel Johnson's life was the 1755 *A Dictionary of the English Language*, which was the standard-bearer for English dictionaries before the *Oxford Dictionary* came out 150 years later. Johnson spent nine years working on the dictionary, combing through other books and compiling more than 100,000 quotations from literary works to demonstrate the meaning of the 42,773 entries within. By taking the time to give the work the effort it deserved, Johnson wrote what was widely considered to be one of the most important books of the century. Just as you can't hurry nature, make sure to give your life's projects the time they deserve. Be patient with yourself.

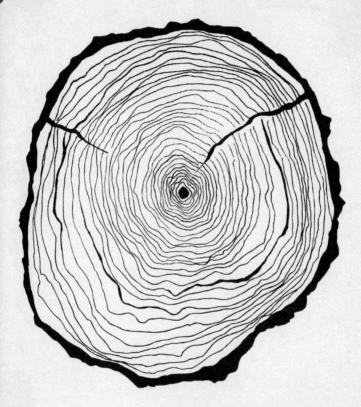

Nature never gives everything at once.

LOOK IN THE MIRROR before you look around you! This quote by Russian writer Leo Tolstoy challenges us to start with ourselves when we want to change the world.

The theme of transforming yourself before you transform what's around you has woven its way into many literary works, political causes, and even songs. Perhaps the most famous espousal of the idea is John F. Kennedy's pivotal line from his 1961 inaugural speech, "Ask not what your country can do for you—ask what you can do for your country." The youngest president ever sworn in—and the first to be born in the 20th century—Kennedy's inauguration was a mental turning point for many young Americans. The line still resonates today, and graces Kennedy's monument at Arlington National Cemetery.

Tolstoy, too, was dedicated to the idea that improving your inner self improves the conditions around you. Work on yourself and the rest will follow.

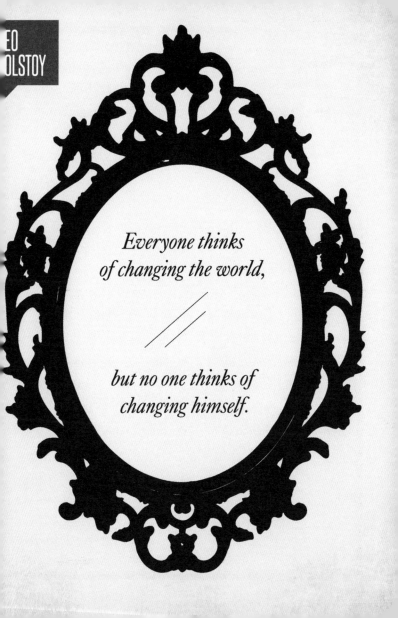

EO
OLSTOY

*Everyone thinks
of changing the world,*

*but no one thinks of
changing himself.*

THE IDEA THAT ART IS JUST IMITATION has been held by some people since the ancient Greeks. Plato wrote about it in his seminal work *The Republic*. But is it? When producing a work of art, the subject matter is filtered through the artist. No matter what the artwork is portraying, how the artist views and interacts with his subject will affect the outcome. Charles Reade wrote plays and stories that highlighted the plight of victims of social injustice. But it's not just writing that is affected by the way its creator sees the world. For example, the brushstrokes a painter uses to draw a hawk flying overhead will change whether he sees the bird as a majestic animal or pities the small creatures it's looking to eat.

The beauty of art is that the individualistic differences don't make artwork less-accurate imitations of the original, but entirely new creations. What illusions, beautiful and otherwise, will you bring to the world with what you create?

CHARLES
READE

ART

IS THERE ANY FEELING MORE JOYOUS than that of experiencing music? Whether you're singing, dancing, or just listening along, music has the ability to lift our spirits and take us away as if we're on the wings of birds.

"Music exalts each joy, allays each grief, / Expels diseases, softens every pain, / Subdues the rage of poison, and the plague," wrote physician and poet John Armstrong. Truly, music can help people feel even more euphoric in times of happiness, and help take them somewhere else when they're experiencing pain or grief. It's even been proven by science—music stimulates more areas of the human brain than anything else we do. But you don't need science to understand how music can make a person feel. Simply put on your favorite song, and let your soul take flight.

*It is a bird-flight of the soul,
when the heart declares itself in song.*

WHY DO WE LOVE OUR PETS SO MUCH?

Could it be that they reflect back the best part of ourselves? Anyone who's spent enough time alone with a dog, cat, or other pet has surely found themselves talking to the animal as if it's a further extension of themselves. Human characteristics can be found in wild animals too—or perhaps, the characteristics of wild animals can be found in us. Victor Hugo's quote (taken from the novel *Les Misérables*) continues, "Animals are nothing but the portrayal of our virtues and vices made manifest to our eyes, the visible reflections of our souls. God displays them to us to give us food for thought." It's impossible not to watch footage of a tiger catching his prey, or a wolf howling at the moon, without feeling a twinge somewhere inside. Is it simply our animal instinct seeing a reflection of itself? When we thank our dogs for greeting us at the door, or shriek when we see a wolf attacking a deer, are we responding to the animals, or to our own inner beings?

All animals are to be found in men and each of them exists in some man, sometimes several at a time.

EVEN WHEN THINGS have gone from bad to worse, you still have the ability to sing, laugh, or love in the small moments you have to yourself.

Peter Gay, an expert on the Enlightenment, wrote this quotation about Voltaire's *Candide*, a famous novella about an optimistic young man who becomes disillusioned after traveling the world. After many wonderful adventures, including spending time in a literal Utopia, Candide ends up unhappily married to the woman he pursued, living at an unremarkable farm in a far corner of the world. However, he's still able to find satisfaction in the hard work of the farm. "Let us cultivate our garden," he tells his companion in the final line of the story. But to Peter Gay, this simple statement meant so much more: "Voltaire has fused the lessons of ancient philosophy into a prescription: Men are thrown into the world to suffer and to dominate their suffering. Life is a shipwreck, but we must not forget to sing in the lifeboats; life is a desert, but we can transform our corner into a garden." What will you plant in your corner?

*Life is a shipwreck
but we must not forget
to sing in the lifeboats.*

THIS QUOTE FROM WILLIAM ARTHUR WARD, one of the English speaking world's most shared and beloved authors of inspiring maxims, reminds us that preparing for what's ahead is more fruitful than complaining about the circumstances that got you there or waiting for them to change on their own.

Just as we have no control over the wind, we have no control over many aspects of our lives. It's hard not to be discouraged when you want your life to go in a certain direction, and you keep getting pulled elsewhere. Instead of getting upset or denying the truth, try adapting to your current circumstances. When you're on a sailboat and the wind is blowing a certain way, it's time to man the pulleys and go with the flow. In life, even small adjustments to match the circumstances around you will take you much further than sitting on the dock and watching the world sail by. Don't forget to always adjust your sails.

WILLIAM
ARTHUR WARD

*The pessimist
complains about the wind;*

*The optimist
expects it to change;*

*The realist
adjusts the sails.*

LEAF OR ARTIST'S PALETTE? This quote from William Hazlitt reminds us that inspiration is all around us, and that all true art comes from our experiences with the world. A painter, writer, and critic, Hazlitt studied with the famous poet William Wordsworth, who he admired for his attention to the beauty of nature. It's said that as Hazlitt observed Wordsworth watching the sunset one night, he remarked, "With what eyes these poets see nature!" Wordsworth not only saw nature differently, he believed in its healing properties, and felt it was important for people to commune with nature so that they could be more grounded in the earth, and, in turn, lead better lives.

Being closer to nature certainly helped Hazlitt—although he lived in many cities throughout his life including London and Paris, he did most of his writing at his bucolic country retreat in a small town in England called Winterslow. How does nature inspire you?

*Art must anchor in nature,
or it is the sport of every breath of folly.*

EVERY DIAMOND IS UNIQUE AND SO STRONG THAT one of the only substances that can scratch it is another diamond. This is because they're formed during billions of years of high pressure deep inside the Earth. Sparkling diamonds are a perfect metaphor for people, who are also hardened by the pressures that formed them.

The duchess in *The Duchess of Malfi*, the play this quote is from, is a person who's been formed by her experience. The play, which premiered at Shakespeare's Globe Theatre in 1613 or 1614, is a fictionalized version of the story of the Italian duchess Giovanna d'Aragona, who went against the wishes of her brothers by remarrying a man below her class. John Webster was a writer of dark tragedies, and *The Duchess of Malfi* is no exception. The duchess's brother Ferdinand imprisons her, telling her, "Whether we fall by ambition, blood, or lust / Like diamonds, we are cut with our own dust."

Our lives are full of diamond-sharp edges. Take pride in the choices you've made and experiences that have shaped you.

Like diamonds,

we are cut with our own dust.

WISDOM COMES FROM EXPERIENCE. Just as a fountain pen needs to be filled with ink in order to write, people need more experiences in order to have the wisdom to create and grow.

Wise people through the ages have prescribed many different kinds of ways to get inspired. Eleanor Roosevelt used to advise, "Do one thing every day that scares you," while others swear by reading books, going for long walks, and the oldest source of inspiration in the book: falling in love. What inspiration do you fill up on, before you create something new?

OMAS
ORE

If with
water you
fill up your
glasses,

You'll
never write
anything
wise.

S A PAINTER ONLY A PAINTER WHEN HE IS PAINTING?

In this quote, Da Vinci opines on the nature of being an artist, whose hands create the universe that's in his mind.

Leonardo Da Vinci was sculptor, architect, inventor, engineer, writer, and geologist, along with a few other professions, but he was best known as the eminent painter responsible for such masterpieces as *The Last Supper* and the *Mona Lisa*. The latter, arguably the most famous painting in the world, contains a spirit that's impossible to peg down, bringing visitors from around the world to the Louvre Museum to view her eyes, which seem to watch you wherever you go. To Leonardo, she represented the quest for perfection, as he kept trying to perfect the painting even after it was finished. Although it was a commissioned work, he never turned it over to its owner, and kept it with him until his death in 1519, sixteen years after he began painting it. There is limitless potential inside each and every one of us. Look inside yourself and find your universe.

*The painter
has the
Universe
in his mind
and hands.*

EVEN THE TALLEST SKYSCRAPERS have to be built piece by piece. When looking at the big picture, don't forget that dreams are achieved step by step—it will take time and effort to get where you're going.

Vincent Van Gogh painted some of the most famous paintings in the world, many of which will still take your breath away up when seen up close. When viewed in person, the works of Van Gogh take on an entirely different meaning and feeling, thanks to the thousands of minute brushstrokes that are often hard to see in reproductions of his work. In Van Gogh's paintings you can see the heaviness of his hand as he moved the brush across the canvas, the texture of the thick oil paints he was creating with, and, when you step back, you can see his entire creation—a starry sky, a café at night, even a simple bedroom—vibrant and alive with the small strokes that have been brought together by Van Gogh's brush. What masterpiece can you create if you realize all ideas start small?

VINCENT
VAN GOGH

Great things

are done

by   *a series*

of small things

brought

together.

HOW DO YOU GET OVER A LOST LOVE? If you're like William Shakespeare's Duke Orsino in *Twelfth Night*, who utters this quote, you listen to music! And you're not alone. Many people say music has inspired them as well as helped them get over a bad break-up. Scientists have discovered that music can cause the brain to release dopamine—the "feel good" chemical that our bodies usually use as a reward for eating and sleeping. For Orsino, music was a way to drown out his sorrows. Just as food sates an appetite, he felt that music could sate his broken heart. "If music be the food of love, play on. / Give me excess of it, that, surfeiting, / The appetite may sicken, and so die," he says. It's unknown if music can completely mend past wounds, but it's impossible to overdose on it. "Play on" and see where it takes you.

WILLIAM
SHAKESPEARE

If music be the food of love, play on.

SOMETIMES WHEN YOU'RE IN THE MIDST of a struggle, it's hard to see that you're fighting for an outcome that will better yourself and everyone around you.

It's Frederick Douglass' vision of the future—his own and his people's—that allowed him to be the accomplished man he was. Born a slave, he escaped to the North and spoke publicly about how badly slaves were being treated in the South. Though he was regularly threatened with being shipping back to the South, where he would be property, he wrote *Narrative of the Life of Frederick Douglass, An American Slave*, his eye-opening autobiography. The victim of violence, arson, and angry mobs throughout his life, Douglass never even thought of being silenced, writing and speaking publicly until his death. In his last speech, he lamented that, although the Civil War seemingly brought freedom to African-Americans, Southern lynch mobs and societal inequities meant the struggle was far from over. Today, it continues, and although sometimes it's easier to see the setbacks than the triumphs, progress is slowly being made. Don't give up the fight! Keep your eyes on the future to gain strength for the present.

FREDERICK
DOUGLASS

If there is no struggle, there is no progress.

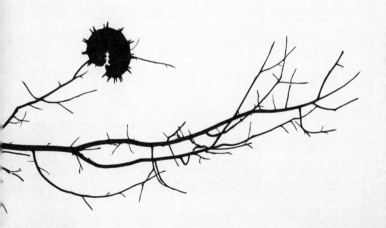

OSCAR WILDE, THE AUTHOR OF MANY PITHY one-liners, reminds us to never be half-hearted in this quote. Wilde himself was known for his life of excess. Called the first person to be "famous for being famous" by David M. Friedman in his book *Wilde in America*, Wilde was known as the outgoing, exuberant person everybody wanted to have at their party. He loved to have a good time and delight friends and strangers with his witticisms, many of which have endured to this day. But it wasn't just fun and games for Wilde—as a gay man in Victorian England, it was dangerous for him to express who he was in the open.

Wilde, however, was unafraid. In 1890, he wrote his masterpiece, *The Picture of Dorian Gray*. It was the first English-language book to openly hint at same-sex desire, and was not only dismissed as filth, but led to Wilde's conviction for "gross indecency" and sentencing to a hard-labor camp for two years. Still, Wilde never regretted being himself, and lives on today as someone known for living life to its fullest. Be unafraid. Be yourself.

Moderation is a fatal thing.

Nothing

succeeds

like

excess.

DO YOU HAVE SOMETHING IN YOUR LIFE THAT'S worth fighting for? This quote from the famous World War II general who was known for inspiring his troops challenges us to be passionate and proud about our beliefs.

George S. Patton is one of the best-known American generals in history for a reason: according to General Wesley K. Clark, Patton's groundbreaking principles about maneuver-based warfare, and combining ground, air, and sea forces forever changed how the US military works—and succeeds—during wartime. But Clark also notes in his foreword to the book *Patton: A Biography* that it was the general's character that made him so revered among soldiers past and present: "He was a winner, a morale- and team-builder who adapted quickly and sought to master every challenge. We need leaders like that today." Do you have the passion to be one of them?

*Better to fight
for something
than live
for nothing.*

HELLO, MY NAME IS RYAN McARTHUR, the artist behind this lovely book that pairs clever quotes with clever visuals. I've always loved quotes because of how much impact they can have in such few words. They can uplift you, make you laugh, make you sad, and can even trigger deep emotions within you. The idea of pairing a quote with a clever illustration came to me throughout my 13 years of advertising. Creating relationships between words and images, making them come together to deliver a message that connects, is truly amazing to me. I want viewers to look at something and at first glance not get it, then get intrigued by it and solve it. There's a self-rewarding payoff there that excites people.

My story is rather simple. I was brought up in a modest household in Southern Ontario, Canada and as far back as I can remember I always appreciated and loved the arts. Starting with crayon on a freshly painted wall, to designing with a mouse and keyboard on a computer screen, I was lucky enough that my artistic abilities gave me the opportunity to pursue a career which I love and can now share with the world. Currently I'm married to my lovely and supportive wife, and together we run around chasing our crazy kids. My days are spent toiling away in my little art shop, "Design Different," where I sell my illustrations to people around the world. Three years ago when I opened my shop I never thought I'd end up being an illustrator sharing my work worldwide, yet here I am writing to you all in my very own book. Be inspired while flipping through the pages of this book. I hope that each quote touches you and connects with you as much as it did for me. The illustrations in this book come from a larger series of prints that can be found online at www.DesignDifferent.ca.